BRING YOUR NIGHTS
WITH YOU

SAINT JULIAN PRESS

POETRY

Praise for BRING YOUR NIGHTS WITH YOU: NEW & SELECTED POEMS, 1975-2015

Thomas Simmons' collected poems are a burning—a wild search of blue flame, the kind with the least oxygen but the most heat, a kind that levels a landscape built on a range of religion, myth, philosophy, erotic intimacy—and aims to rebuild it with the act of looking at it with clear eyes.

From the shut-in child who says, "I began to calculate the area … of my life" and "how much I had, in inches, millimeters, feet," to the reveling in the grown body's hidden ecstasies and "the rightness of the body in its rightful place," Simmons' poetry contains a watchfulness that is complicated by its own act of watching. It is a watchfulness aware of its failings, which vacillates from an undistracted mission—such as Muhammed who, with the "tunnel vision" of religious fervor, only sees "out of the corner of his eye, the child Ayesha uncupping her hands and lifting the butterflies aloft"—to the full acknowledgement that any understanding comes beyond language, like the father and the child who take a wordless walk in the snow and discover "it had been enough, the sound / Of boots in the snow, the quiet, the sudden sun, Her hand in his."

Simmons examines how human experience is best understood with tools outside of language, outside the relentless pursuit of assigning sign to signifier. There he says, we can find among the wreckage, "the beauty of it: my own circular ruins." For it is the not "hard words that we train for" but its subsequent weighty silences, the aftermath, and after reading it, one is left haunted and unsettled by images—such as the child shaking in his loft bed during a hurricane busily loosening the rafters of his house—images that silence our chatter-filled mind as we recognize it, unfailingly, as ourselves.

—Leslie Contreras Schwartz, author of
Fuego and *Nightbloom & Cenote*

Thomas Simmons is rumored to have said, "It's in the nature of the human for trances to be broken. It's in the nature of the divine for trances to be trances. The human doesn't cancel the divine—just re-directs for a time."

His two volumes of poetry represent decades of trance, as the collection flows in and out of re-direction and return, and as Simmons successfully mediates between subject of casual cognizance and participant observation of his own experience.

The poems in *Bring Your Nights With You* must have been strenuously hand-picked to accomplish the unexpected calling on the reader to arrive authentically at the work, *without mythologies*, yet to also leave the page with a sense of dogma, *just there, that new synaptic link, that thing, meaning*, arguably just as genuine as the consistent call here to re-learn the workings of light versus the unseen. We trust there is balance and truth in the path Simmons unveils before us, and there is.

A must-read for those caught in the liminal space without the desired benefit of *night goggles*.

—Rachel Sutcliffe, singer-songwriter, Cedar Rapids, Iowa

BRING YOUR NIGHTS WITH YOU

New and Selected Poems,
1975-2015

Thomas Simmons

Volume Two

SAINT JULIAN PRESS
HOUSTON

Published by
SAINT JULIAN PRESS, Inc.
2053 Cortlandt, Suite 200
Houston, Texas 77008

www.saintjulianpress.com

ISBN-13: 978-1-7320542-1-9
ISBN: 1-7320542-1-5
Library of Congress Control Number: 2018939161

Cover Art & Design: Thomas Simmons & Ron Starbuck
Author Photo: Ron Starbuck

FOR MY CHILDREN—NATE, GEORGIA,
THOMAS, HART, PETER, AND FAYE—
WITH LOVE ALWAYS

CONTENTS

Volume Two

<u>BETRAYAL</u>

DECEMBER 18, 2010, 4:30 P.M.   3
SOLIPSISM   4
TOMORROW WILL BE DELAYED   5
FELINE FERAL FULL   6
MEMORIAL   7
BETRAYAL   8
JIHAD   9
UNBETROTHED   10
IOWA ORDINARY   11
STAR LIGHT, STAR BRIGHT   12
BETHLEHEM   13
CHRISTMAS TREE   14
THE ELEMENTS   15
DISAPPOINTMENT   16
THE MAGIC ROOM   17
APOLOGY   18
THANKSGIVING DAY, 1988   19
EYE OF THE STORM   20
KEYS, LIDS, ACID, SPEED   21
DARK ROOM   23
FORTUNE-TELLING   24
THE MONUMENT   25
FINDING ONE'S WAY   26
OUTSIDE MY WINDOW   27
A CANINE LANGUAGE   28
KEEPING UP   30
THE END OF ILLUSION   31
TIRED SOUL   33
HERE AND NOW   34
THE BLUE HOUR   35
ON WISHING TO HAVE BEEN ABORTED   36
THE NIGHT   38

BRING YOUR NIGHTS WITH YOU

TO THE HARBORMASTER   43

A SHADOW ON THE MOON   44

DARK WING   45

AFTER DRINKING ALL NIGHT
WITH A FRIEND, I GO OUT
IN A BOAT AT DAWN
TO SEE WHO CAN WRITE THE BEST POEM   46

THE FIRST NIGHT   47

POEM FOR MY BIRTHDAY, JUNE 11, 2011   48

SPARE POEM   49

IN THE ASCENDANT   50

ANTICIPATION   51

FOR A YOUNG CHILD WHO PUT
A FLASHLIGHT IN THE FREEZER   52

THE HISTORY OF REST   53

GRACE   54

NIGHT RIDE HOME   55

WHAT THEY FOUND
UNDER THE STRAW
IN A STALL
OF THE ABANDONED BARN   56

THE FORMALISTS   57

THE REVELATION   58

CHRISTMAS NOTE TO SELF   59

UNREAL CITY   60

THE SECRET PLACE OF THE MOST HIGH   61

COMING ABOUT   62

UNSTOPPABLE   63

SADNESS, ITS NATURAL HISTORY   64

PRIVACY   65

THE POEM OF FURTHEST MEMORY   66

OH MY HEART   67

INTERLUDE: AUBADE   68

THIS POEM, MY HAND, THE BOOK   69

THINGS I REMEMBER   70

THE NAMES OF THE LOST   71

WAITING   72

WHATEVER IT IS   73

BLACK DRESS JEAN JACKET   74

COLD   75

DEPRESSION SPEAKS ON THE EVE
OF ITS TWENTIETH ANNIVERSARY   76
AND THEN YOU   77
LIKE KITTENS   78
NAVY   79
BRING YOUR NIGHTS WITH YOU   80
LANDSCAPE   81
GARDEN PARTY   82
CHELSEA HOTEL NUMBER   83
GRANITE   84
RESIDUUM   85
SIGHTINGS   86
THE INTERRUPTION   87
CHANGES   88
NEAR THE END   89

"I stayed with Fortunata for one month, learning more about her ways and something about my own. She told me that for years she had lived in hope of being rescued; of belonging to someone else, of dancing together. And then she had learned to dance alone, for its own sake and for hers.

'And love?' I said.

She spread her hands and gave me a short lecture on the habits of the starfish."—Jeanette Winterson,
Sexing the Cherry (1989)

BRING YOUR NIGHTS
WITH YOU

BETRAYAL

DECEMBER 18, 2010, 4:30 P.M.

Now the pale earth falls by the side of the road
And the long shadows acquire the authority of night.

This is no season. Winter is an irrelevance.
The cold is an inert fact, like matter.

How solid things look—the houses, the cars.
The trees. The grey rose bush beside the aluminum siding.

To witness all this happening again, the hardness
Of things, the sureness of illusion, and its death:

The feeling in the hardness of bones that the point
Is elsewhere, in the darkness, and much later, in the light.

SOLIPSISM

Later in the evening, listening to the sound
His soul made splashing against the dark window,
He detected, for the first time, another sound,

As of the rain if there had been any. The rain
And his soul cavorted on the fluid panes
As he watched, entranced, all the while knowing

This was an ending of some kind, *kenosis,* an emptying,
Ironic for all the plenitude around. How to say good-bye
When one has already gone? In the quiet he no longer cared.

TOMORROW WILL BE DELAYED

A Lullaby

Everyone has a bad day. Tonight
It will be yours to lay in the snowlight

Of old sorrow, flake by flake, in the amber
Moon, then faster, streak by streak, past number

Anyone could count—that is the way of sorrow,
No? It eludes the strategy that says: "I know.

My sorrow is yours." Empathy is not enough.
But we work with dour weather, and the rough

Discipline of moving in the beautiful drifts of amber
We did not ask for. Drift, now, and do not remember.

FELINE FERAL FULL

For DWK

Tornado alley and the cats are skittish. Nights now
We ride NOAA and unseen cerulean seas of cloud.
Wild, wild. . .The two, last of some litter: ruined
In the field, eight weeks maybe, hardwired for fear
But brilliant. They know: nothing to learn beyond
Lean survival, which would be how they learned me.
But see how the storm looms invisible and the sirens
Go off and on, too traumatized to care. . . .Cowering
By my side but not for love I swear: my doomed body
shelters theirs. I arise. *What is love?* I ask the mirror
And the mirror goes black. Too late: yet there it is.

MEMORIAL

"I am living, I remember you"—that affirmation
Of the moment and, instantly, the memory, the link
Between the living and the dead. The best that we can do,
Bringing the dead back time and again into the brief eternity
Of the present, laying them out like transparencies across
The panorama of the real. This is Marie Howe, in "Memorial,"
At the window of the local video store. Or: "The dead are made
Of bronze. But dying they were like birds with clock-like hearts."
Does every poet have a poem "Memorial"? Here, Robert Pinsky,
An image taken not just from a specific memory, but from "bird,"
"Clock-like," and "heart," not common together. Bob Hass
In "Meditation at Lagunitas": *"blackberry, blackberry, blackberry."*
An SOS. I had a very brilliant student recently, an expert
In semiotics, who argued against the history of memory
From William James to Tony Damasio to Eric Kandel,
Countering that since the images of memory no more refer
To anything outside themselves than any other semiotic,
Memory cannot be the core site of the autobiographical self.
Even this poem, of course, in such a light turns out not to refer
To anything but its own play of signs and how, as on a city bus
Or plane, they might bump up against your own play of signs.
Parallel play, the first thing children do as strangers.
Should we wonder at our loneliness? Adrift in fictions, we forge
The stories we either believe or disbelieve, and tell them,
Over and over, making them real. Two weeks ago at midnight
An old man came out of John's Market, stammering to no one,
Help me, please, I need someone to help me, not looking up,
Not making eye contact, not reaching for an arm or a hand, and so
No one did anything. If only he had touched one of us, or we
Had touched him, it might all have been different. Now he, too,
Is a story where, in a moment, he might have been a memory
Uncontrolled by semiotics, a frighteningly true thing.

BETRAYAL

Snow in the yard, now mostly gone:
Frozen rivulets of filthy, mottled ice
Unmoored from beauty, unsummarizable,

Leaving us again among the dead
Of winter—not the frozen ground
Merely, but the sense of betrayal,

Having given ourselves over to what was cold
And beautiful, only to have it snatched away
Once more, as if all our daughters were

Persephone, and all our grievings infuriatingly
Trivial, never enough, though we might become
Terrorists of the earth in our aimless vengeance.

JIHAD

The temptation is to fight. And there is
A holy beauty to violence in a certain light,
The insanity of a desert in flames, bathed
In ebony oil, too far beyond comprehension
To elude the beautiful, or the man on fire,
Unstoppable, the gorgeousness of what cannot
Be restrained. Against this the beautiful refuge
Is powerless, mute bystander before the flame.
So it is that one must choose. . .Rather like
Faith, or a question of faith, or perhaps
A question of the divine. It is the easiest thing
In the world to overwhelm the divine,
If it exists. It is powerless. Its beauty
Demands that one decide, and though
It is not an illusion, exactly, the fact
That it may be real only at the moment
Of one's choosing is a source of infinite
Distress. Choose the refuge, and it is
There, or not, and one constructs the beauty
One intuitively craves. Or blows it apart.
Either way, something, if only a shard
Of a soul or a corner of the heart, remains.

UNBETROTHED

At the altar of the little church,
On a Wednesday, he moved softly,
As if touching a down comforter,
Or a child's cheek in sleep—the white linen,
Candlesticks, the wax of the candles,
The chalice. Where were the people?
They had been here, once, on a late morning,
Somewhat hungover, but, coming into possession
By the place itself, in earnest: I do, I do,
The ritual by which such objects spring to life,
Becoming piece and anchor of those lives. . .
Voyeur, coming back to look, to touch, as if
It could be done again, as if any word
Or touch were good enough, yet knowing
The urgency of the desire here, in this place,
Unseen, not like a child's tale, but an adult's.

IOWA ORDINARY

The familiar, executed without thought, nevertheless
Becomes the object of the most minute fascination:
The radiance of the yellow center, the slightly viscous,
Technically-misnamed egg "white" sliding into the little river
Of milk, the intricately-chopped onion, the vivid meat,
And the kneading, over and over, the feel of it all
Squeezed through your fingers till the spread is even,
And the loaf in the pan requires only its hot oven
And a certain squiggle of ketchup over the top.
Dinner happens because you make it happen,
The pleasure of doing sequentially without thinking,
As if what David Hume said about God, demolishing
The theory of design, must apply, at times, to you, too:
Your own creation unpremeditated, no rift between thought
And action, and the possibility that thus you, too, were
For a moment alien to the creation, a different kind of being,
You and God, from all others who think first, and then act.

STAR LIGHT, STAR BRIGHT

For Christopher Merrill

The first flower
Of the first earth
In its first age
Child of the sea
Anemone opening,
Closing in the deeper
Wave, aging, released
Finally to be singular
Within the current,
Moving over millennia
Into veins of tiny animals,
Mammoth in arctic ice,
Caves of women and men,
And on up and finally out
Through blue to black
And the enormous patience
Of light in the heavens,
Kinsman, finally, at home,
Still seeming to speak
Through the tremulous atmosphere,
Saying: Wishing is in your blood,
Your bones, you cannot stop,
It is what takes you up and out
At last, whether or not
There is an answer
To your desire
Out here everything
Answers to desire

BETHLEHEM

The ten thousandth year came and went
Unremarked: soirées gathered their kind,
Poets wrote, and politicians of dubious note
Plied their ambiguous warfare. Astronomers
Turned to the night sky and their own equations,
Seeking gravitational curios, that long lure
Of extra-terrestrial life. Familiar to the bedlamite,
The parapet remained unassailed, though bombs
Exploded in city centers and trucks plowed into crowds.
Because increasingly life took place on the tablet screen
Or some other virtual space, the handful who noticed
The passing of the date, January 1, 2017, had nothing
To tell anyone, not even one another. It was enough
That they knew. That much had been passed down,
Published from time to time—the most recent
Valentin Tomberg, 1985, twelve years after his death;
Before that, 1939, in the same year Yeats himself died.
How it had always been: the ages transforming themselves
With or against the people, the people later at war
Or peace, betrayed, hoping without hope, alone
At the end. And still it all became as it was to be,
That larger dream of which each night-bound vision
Derives its minor sliver, its demon-children.

CHRISTMAS TREE

Excessive obligation and exhaustion have made it
Impossible to take down, and so it has come to seem
Part of the furniture, the magical part like Robert
Pinsky's figured wheel, with little chimes and bells
Of many pitches, rolling on its circumferential light
Around the otherwise dark and silent living room,
Brittle as a Grecian urn. Touch it, and the shower
Of needles is a warning: one spark and this will turn
To a truer illumination, and deadlier. But as it takes
Root here, in its odd, uncapturable way, it offers
The illusion that magic is anywhere, in a tiny glass
Schoolhouse, or a pear with one forlorn leaf
Still attached from whenever it was my mother
Purchased it, perhaps in 1956. The colored balls
Are translucent from the years. Horrifying my father,
Who spent his life imagining fires everywhere and trying,
Over and over, to put them out, my mother would leave
The tree up till Valentine's Day, as an omen for the year.
Fragile tree, frozen in time, with lights from the past
And nimble as a torch, it would grace the house beneath
My father's seethings. The first year ever we took it
Down before Valentine's was the year my mother died.

THE ELEMENTS

"It sounds like a bell buoy out at sea.
It is the elements speaking: earth, air, fire, water."
—Elizabeth Bishop, "In the Village"

That day, rowing a mile off Swans Island
In an eight-foot skiff just to prove I could,
High swells, and in the end a lobster boat
Named "Pegasus," but not pronounced that way,
Veering off from his traps to see if I was OK,
It struck me that the Gooseberry Ledge buoy was,
And wasn't, what it was: Yes, it marked the turn
Toward Burnt Coat Harbor, that first crucial sign.
But in its groan it seemed, finally, self-referential,
Telling a story not made by hands to a world not made
By hands. Earth, air, fire, water, the buoy groaning. . .
It would not really matter if we were not here,
Except that, being here, we must tell what it is
We see and thus, almost by accident, change it,
Changing ourselves and our places, though
On their own they go on and on, speaking
To themselves, not as if we didn't matter,
But as if their own discourse were so essential
We were, in the end, a kind of afterthought.
I sat for a few minutes, in the Atlantic
In a boat almost too small to see, waving
The lobsterman off, though he turned a slow turn,
As if disbelieving. Just to float, to hear the sound
Of the handful of stories I could never decipher,
All around. Of course, it was a long row back.

DISAPPOINTMENT

The ugliest emotion, even worse than envy
Or jealousy, because so intimately linked to hope,
The lover's familiar, the way things might have been
And thus a kind of alternative universe: in this
Universe of hope, one's intuitions, even one's
Fantastic projections, meld into the real,
And one lives a waking dream, knowing oneself awake.
Disappointment is like sleepwalking in a world
Of ash: touch the beautiful and it crumbles,
Touch the lovely and it dwindles, touch hope,
And it laughs derisively and turns away, lively
And loud with others, or an other, at a hotel bar.
Walk down an Edward Hopper street, toward the diner
Where the lonely lights are on, but light at least:
You reach for the door handle but it too turns
To ash. Touch nothing, no one.

THE MAGIC ROOM

For A.D.

Open the ordinary door. Be brave. At first
It is all darkness. Then a kind of umber comes,
As if dawn were a brune from above, and then
A kind of daylight comes through the windows
That are not there. A man and a woman are seated
At a table. They have lost a child. Unbelieving,
You touch them, caressing their sad cheeks,
And your love comforts them in a way unspeakable,
For only you and I know that I have brought you here.
You have entered their story, a story without words,
Just as you requested. You see, the room itself affirms:
This is how it is done. In the next room, a child
Is asleep in her deepest dreams. You carry her
To the grieving woman and place her in her hands,
And suddenly there is incomprehensible joy,
A miracle, which you yourself performed, how
They will never know. Without asking you the room
Nevertheless says, What do you want, and you say
Pluto, and suddenly you are there, you and the Little
Prince, walking without atmosphere over the terrain
From which the earth is no longer visible.
"Apprivoiser," the Little Prince is saying.
"To tend, to care for." What you learned here
When you first arrived, years before now.
On the other side is, inevitably, the other door
And, taking your deepest breath, you step out
Into an Iowa City day. But at least I could show you
It was true, this magic room, and always here.
And I was glad to be there, for a time, with you.

APOLOGY

Hard enough in a day to know oneself
Even provisionally—how much harder then
To believe one's knowledge of others, to trust
That what one has said, or not said, or otherwise

Implied will be read with any accuracy, any
Clarity at all? We are taught apology
From childhood, too often with enforced shame,
And worse, we learn in anger that some things

Cannot be taken back—though merely words
They blossom into myths of cruelty wreathing
Our heads and memories. The only hope lies
In revision: Dante has Paolo and Francesca

Circle each other for eternity, never again
To touch, no tolerable apology for infidelity.
The premise of hell is unforgiveness. Yet, in his
Late rendering of the *Inferno,* William Blake

Illuminates the circle as it was but then
Restores the two of them off to the side,
Their ecstatic ascent, recognizing, as Dante
Did not, the beatitude of passion past the lie.

THANKSGIVING DAY, 1988

Escaping the crucible of Massachusetts,
We arrived at my sister's Maine island,
Seven hours of child-punctured silences
And the refuge of a fifty-minute
Ferry ride. That day, an old man
(Old by my standards then; my age now)
Came into the harbor in a sixteen-foot
Centerboard sailboat, mainsail and jib,
With a bit of canvas over the bow
For a kind of cabin. He was sailing
Around the world. News crossed
The small island quickly: by afternoon,
He was at our house for Thanksgiving.
What could he offer, he wondered aloud,
As a gift for this gift? A sail around
The harbor? My sister, with her
Twenty-one foot Corinthian, frowned.
The water was 38 degrees. If we capsized,
We'd freeze before we drowned. Kindly,
She refused. But I said yes. And it was
A great sail, strong winds, and cold,
As if we were on the way to Troy,
Or just setting out for home. And there was
One frozen moment, the great gust
And the boat heeling mast-close
To the water, heedless water coming up
At us—but then recovery, that righting.
When we returned, the tension in the house
Was such that all the lights were on. Afterward
I was not less-loved, or shunned, but treated
With respect, at first, and later, now, with caution.

EYE OF THE STORM

The noise is deafening, but the light is beautiful.
The shafts from heaven burn with scintillation
though across the half-troubled waters is a wall
Of blackness in every direction. A million birds
Circle aimlessly, in that distracted state that exceeds
Panic, gulls, terns, whatever got swept up and still
Survived. It is a vertical tunnel, with a tunnel's
Terrible, incessant noise, the whitewashed sound
Of internally-justified motion to no end. This vessel
Pitches and rolls as if it were accustomed to extremity,
Which, though it is, was not a laminate laplaid
With human hands. Still, you have to have come
Through one side into this. You will go on into
The other at some point. But will you? At present
You outrun the storm. The roar of the other side,
Inconceivably, grows louder. The swells rise.
You stand mute and alone at the helm.
The worst is knowing what is already there.

KEYS, LIDS, ACID, SPEED

*"And now that the great sweep of the acid years is over, I cannot unlearn the
things that I learned during them, I cannot deny the vision of what the world
might be like. Everything that we glimpsed—the trust, the brotherhood, the
repossession of innocence, the nakedness of spirit—is still a possibility and will
continue to be so."*

*—Thom Gunn, "My Life
Up to Now"*

A young woman is staring at an old-fashioned
Digital clock with little metal plates of numbers
That flip, once a minute, in a glow of red.
The red fills the room, her gaze, the inside
Of her head. She can see her brain, now a rose.
Each time a minute goes, the world starts over,
Lovelier than before. For a whole night,
Darkness around her, she stares entranced
Until, by morning, she is in an ecstasy of love
For a world made indescribably beautiful
In four hundred and eighty separate
Transformations. When I meet her,
Years later, this is one of the first stories
She tells, by way of saying, should you care
To know me, you will need to know
This about me, this thing that formed me
When I was twenty, that I would never
Let you do because I know already you
Would never make it back. Divisive,
This power of vision, although it might
Have easily gone the opposite way,
But an ordinary day is undergirded
With quiet conflict and subterranean agendas
So subtle they elude detection apart from
The telepathy of soul to soul, and those souls
Mutely turn away, diurnal disappointment
Having come to be their breakfast and their supper.
Really, it is a wonder they endure as fiercely
As they do. Still, they were born from the red light
Of the mind in an ecstasy of emergence,
Knowing instantly that they were also
Never born, co-existent with the non-beginning,

Always destined to go home, and always home.
Burn away the day like the morning fog
On Cole Street just off the Haight
In San Francisco, and you get the vision,
The certainty, the certain hand held out to you.
But it is a hard thing for one man
Alone to burn away the fog.

DARK ROOM

Yes, it was.   There was one door
        and one armchair. It was   the farthest back   room
           in the pasha's palace   for when the bombs   fell.

He wanted to hear   a word for each thing
        each state   and he wanted instantaneously
           to know it.   *"Mais l'exercice essential*

du compositeur—la meditation—rien ne la jamais
        suspendu en moi."   *La meditation.*
          The dark.   Muffled   something

from the bar becoming   over time   simply that—
       a word that did not exist.   Love—no—
          metempsychosis—yes.   Sound—no.

Or: hydrogen and oxygen becoming water—that sound.
        Yes. When it became   possible   to hear
          at the sub-atomic level   it did not

cloud his head   insanely   as the fly buzzing
        at the point of death.   It was the point of death
          but it was not—dying—it was as things were

Just after the very beginning—immeasurably fast—pure
       sensation.   And the quiet.   Absolute quiet.
       And then   he knew.

And he got up: rejoined the crowd.

FORTUNE-TELLING

In Memory of J. V. Cunningham

Nothing will make amends
For bitterness that extends
Past three lost years, and mourns

The way a certain realm of love ends;
Not true, but faithful, it contends
Unsteadily with rumours it intends

Somehow to betray, and though that lie
Is known in time, the portents must say
Otherwise. Fortune-teller, I must lay

The lie aside to wake now justified, while she
Who has another wakens with simple ease,
Somewhat more beloved, more appeased.

THE MONUMENT

Still there, despite the decades past or more—
That strange dilapidation of wooden cubes,
Leaning toward trapezoidal though each segment
Roughly resistant, the nails slowly compromising—
And the pier as well, not yet severed from land
Though the storms have come and will come
And here and there some creosoted planks
Have in their way consented to the waves.
What way is "in their way"? I cannot tell,
Not because I am withholding but because
I simply do not know. And yet this postcard
Annotates the seemingly pointless structure
And, implicitly, the way to it. You can visit.
To do what? It is too cold in winter, otherwise
Too hot, and no amenities: no one knows
Why. It might have as well have been built
Inside Lascaux. Price's Hotel burned
At Pleasure Bay almost a century ago,
And so passed the opera there, the tenor
Pouring out his depths. . .When we do that,
That is when we reach *the friable edge*: one
Root of our devotion is our mortal sorrow
That good-bye already lurks in gas lines,
In the furnace and the careless match. *Never
The same way twice, or twice and again,
Ranging and building,* yet see now how
That old construction still demands its place—
As if the builder knew its native home
Was multiple, in wood and nails but also
In these, Elizabeth's and Al's words, Robert's,
Mine. . .No such luck for Price's Hotel, but then
It served a different purpose. Here you are,
And here I am. Here and there Theo Jansen's
Strandbeests are doing precisely this, merely
Adding fragility and motion, although
Here not a thing is fragile or still. Burn this,
And the ash becomes the cenotaph of what endures.

FINDING ONE'S WAY

Awakening in the dark, after a night
Of fitful sleep, one becomes aware,
Slowly, of a certain shift, as if the room
Were one's own room but invisibly
Rearranged. The temptation is,
Not to stand up, but to reach out.
The first touch draws blood;
One cannot see it but feels the sting,
The dampness running down the palm.
The second touch, too, draws blood.
The third touch is something like
A pillow, or a cushion—a sofa, perhaps,
But turned sideways, like a barricade.
It is a maze, lined with blades of all kinds,
Knives, razors, small and large, and the rotten
Little box-cutters. All unseen. Crawling,
Alert to the slightest, invisible aura of metal,
Still one feels the hot wound on one's arms,
Ribs, thighs, calves, and worst of all, face,
A passion without love, a yearning against
All wounding, a negative with no positive
Except the exit, which must, at last, be somewhere.
It is there, a door. One opens it and finds
The strangest thing was not the trauma,
Or the inexplicability of it—how, after all,
Did one get there?—but the contrast:
Daylight, cars, and buses, and the people
Glancing away and stepping aside, as if
One were homeless, or spare change.

OUTSIDE MY WINDOW

Last night, in dreams, someone I loved was slowly
Killing herself upstairs, and something restrained me:
I was powerless to help. They wrapped her body
In Saran Wrap and lowered her down. Awakening,
I found myself pulling at the sheets, the pillows,
Making sure they were real, and mine,
As if that were truly confirmation. Now,
At work all day indoors, and looking out the window
At the surge of traffic and the people with their dogs,
It seems strange to me that violence is intrinsic
To our being, when what seems the most violent
Is more like stepping through plate glass—
The terrible shock, insuperable pain, then the discovery
That the next thing, the other world, whatever
You want to call it, was waiting there all along,
Neither indifferent nor different to you, or if
Different, in a familiar way, as if you had just
Disembarked from a bloodied bus, in horror,
And no one turned or cared, though no one
Was hostile, either—just there, just there, until
The horror, too, began to seem like a dream.

A CANINE LANGUAGE

"Cut loose, without devotion, a man becomes a comic."
          —Marie Howe, "Without Devotion"

You are lonely. I am lonely, too. But this is the era
Of social media, and thus we will never meet. However:

Today I am remembering the animal shelters, in Iowa City
And in West Chester, Pennsylvania, and the dog breeders,

Always out in the country, not remote exactly but easily
          overlooked.
The noise. The chaos. Sometimes the pens, sometimes just the straw

In the barn. Strays. Abandoned. Or the litter: the little ones
Dashing around, nipping each other, and the one who comes over,

And scarcely moves when you pick her up, and doesn't want to be
Set down, and if you do lays herself across your foot until

You pick her up again. One body utterly sure of the other, and the other
Suddenly sure. You say *yes*. And we wonder how it is difficult to talk

About love, about knowing. So much language. . .When the body speaks,
Secretly, in its own voice, nothing needs to be said. *Refusing translation.*

Metaphysics. How things "seem" one way but portend another,
How "this" reality is contingent, accidental, but the Platonic Forms

Endure forever. How we must argue for the primacy of the
          transcendent.
No. You pick up the one puppy across your foot and then you never

Let go, and she never lets go, and after that, when people talk
          about love,
You go silent. This is the reality that began with the Devonian,

When nothing spoke, not the trilobites, not the crinoids swaying
In the shallow sea. The world was the world, with nothing to imagine,

A world in love unaware with itself. Yet each being discrete. Late

You awaken and the puppy is there, growing now in the proverbial leaps
     and bounds,

But asleep, curled in beside you. *What We Talk About When We Talk
About Love*—meaning something else, something not-love—akin

To Andreas Capellanus. Liars. Abelard, but not Heloise. One body
Embodies itself, and another responds. The girl with the degree

In metaphysics is a false voice, her teacher a liar. She knows that.
If her body never learned to cover another and stay with it

Outside of time, it was not for absence of love, but for
The presence of language, that vice between the sheets.

KEEPING UP

Slowly, although I dust and mop and do the dishes
Almost daily, the house has the feel of a place
Receding into the earth—a reality for which,
Presumably, I should be grateful, for there is
No house that is not mortal. Yet some endure,
Flourish, acquire new coats of paint or new
Vinyl siding; mine gently, irrevocably
Disintegrates. Perhaps the mindset
Is inherited—I mean the mind of the house,
Transmuted through the owner: once,
When I was a child and we were trying
To sell our house in Pennsylvania,
A realtor said it was so filthy no one
Would consider buying it. My mother
Sat down on the stairs and cried.
What I remember most about her
Were the days when she would lock herself
In her room—two days, three at a time.
The house would be very quiet, then.
My father would place trays of food
By the door, and speak softly to her,
Then go to work, and later return.
We kids were on our own. Then
It was a great mystery; now, I think,
I understand. Sometimes one needs
To sink into the element one is supposed
To exclude, which is after all one's own:
Reconciling to this is very private,
And a form of grief, like housekeeping.

THE END OF ILLUSION

Hard by the caverns beneath the huge hall
Of the 1666 post-Civil Wars mansion
With its four stories, rose garden hidden
Behind the twelve-foot-high rectangular hedge
With its secret door, the carriage houses,
Tea room, the dank but novel swimming pool,

180 acres of formal gardens and crafty
Wilderness and, yes, the tunnels out
To the Thames, all straight from history
And Central Casting, a man was perfecting
Illusion. It was a years-long project,
Not initially intended or designed,

Something to keep him occupied
Given his modest independent wealth,
And he kept a journal. At first
It was simple tricks—the right card
From the deck, a rabbit out of a hat.
Then came the problem of disappearance:

Also a trick, at first, but he had studied
Elizabeth Bishop's "One Art" as a
Gnostic text, and came to understand,
If he concentrated long enough and called
On fate, he could conjure an image
Of what was just on the verge of being lost.

Once, three years into the project,
He concentrated all night on the game
Warden for the estate; that next morning,
No—he lay dead in the service elevator.
Then there was no turning back. He studied
Science and Health with Key to the Scriptures

To perfection, and from his terrible basement
He could move objects five flights up,
Change the influenzas of the staff to health,
Make the long-dead Jaguar run. People began
To talk of a new miracle worker, unlikely
As always, the old recluse at Cliveden,

But even as they spoke and began,
On Sundays, to gather in the Great Hall,
Not to entreat him, for he never emerged,
But to see if something needed would happen—
No, by then he had given up. For he saw
That no change really took: the miracles

For which he garnered local fame in no way
Altered how the people lived, or moved,
Or had their being. They were grateful
Temporarily, yet more the same. It was
The setness of things, the imperviousness,
Despite the often-professed love of change,

That shook him. In his journal his last entries
All were about the last chapters of Brett Millier's
Biography of Bishop, all about *Geography III*,
And often about "Five Flights Up." Last trick:
He poured a bowl of vodka for himself, transformed
Into a dog, and drank. And that is how they found him:

Down by the Thames, near the cottage where
The game warden had lived, the howling
Of a lone wolf terrifying the populace
Who of course called the local constabulary.
They could not capture him alive. But it took them
A long time to comprehend what they had snuffed out.

TIRED SOUL

True, it is not only the care
You carry with you from afar
Or the what-if's hurtling anywhere

But the accumulations of the actual
From near, and earlier, and still
Further back, the mortal everywhere.

Useless to suggest rest, in your case,
Though that is what you need, unless
You can unlearn the insomniac's caress:

Refuse to massage what is unfixable,
And quest, late nights, for the fragile
Oblivion that is your special tale,

The unforgiven's one great story,
No beginning, middle, end, yet any
Who hear may be disturbed at being sorry.

HERE AND NOW

One day, not so long from now,
You will not remember that,
When you were tired, you would lie
Next to me in bed with a nippled
Bottle of chocolate milk, and stroke
My hair, over and over, as I said,
Softly, "Daddy's head, Daddy's hair,"
While we watched *Kipper,* a late '90s
British show about a happy dog and friends.

Other memories, and life lived, the footballs
You can catch as well as throw, intense
Imaginings, the lives of the tiny people
You've already begun to drive around
In Matchbox cars—all this will crowd
The earliest memories, reducing them
At best to a faint intuition, unnamed feeling.
I leave these temporal words to prove
To myself, this time, this reality of love.

THE BLUE HOUR

Perhaps what is needed is a small altar
With tapered candles, incense,
And an icon of the Blessed Virgin,
Or Her Son, or something utterly ambiguous,
Unnamable figure made sacred only
By its centrality. Then, in sickness
And isolation, loathing the consciousness
That moves me through the darkened,
Almost disembodied house, I would myself
Become half-disembodied, swept up
In the small flame and the fragrant smoke
To the place that no one knows, which after all
Can scarcely be much different from the air
Inside the house, the air outside, the stratosphere,
Or the vacuum where the stars work their
Invisible gravitation. If I gravitate, at this hour,
Toward one who is not here, it is because
We may well be elsewhere, in some other
Life, not as ourselves, but selves who know
The thin shafts of light that bind us
And prevent us here, selves embodied
In something a bit like smoke, and fire,
Always gravitating toward an altar.

ON WISHING TO HAVE BEEN ABORTED

One approaches it with great caution and a certain expertise

The way one would approach unexploded ordnance from WWII

In a field outside London. . .Still, there it is, in her imperfect

Penmanship, her blue ink, the diary entries from 1955—

What bothered her was not any question of life or not-life,

Since as a Christian Scientist she didn't really believe in "the body"

Anyway, although like everyone in the family she went nuts

Over sex—no, what bothered her was that it was illegal.

So close. . .Then the subject completely vanishes.

                                        At an after-reading dinner

In Houston one Bastille Day, I was seated next to a prominent TV anchor,

Who admired my poems. Quite a bit in them is explicit,

Implicitly. She asked: "But if you had it all to do again,

Knowing what you know now, so you would see the mistakes

From far off and so could avoid them, wouldn't you?" I said—

No hesitation—"Oh, no. I would never live this life again. Ever."

Her shock took me aback, a little. And I think of my poor children

Reading this. . . But we don't know that genetics actually explain

All of causality, how in your different ways all six of you

Might nevertheless have been fine. . .No, in the end

Because the subject is so complicated it comes down to a miserly

Cost-benefit analysis: Were the good things, the children, the poems,

The students, worth the terrible losses, the worst of which I have

To drink away each night, they stay so close. . .And in the end

The answer is simply "No." I know. And how, in "real time,"

To think of the rising generation as if they could be anyone

But who they are, as if their same mothers with that "other" father

Would be just as good, or better, or whether perhaps they chose

each place they hold from the place *where we go in sleep,* as Robert

       Pinsky said. . .

The British poet George Jisho Robertson, a profound Buddhist, believes

We can talk to the unborn as we talk to the dead—there is no rupture

In the stream, only the illusion. Parts of his argument are captivating, but I

Wouldn't want to be bothered. I think we only talk to the dead or the unborn

If they wish to talk to us. My mother, who died in 1980, has never

Wished to make contact. For others of the dead I know, and some I don't,

Who know me, talking is as simple as changing the parameters of the room.

THE NIGHT

Everywhere at night there are mirrors
Of the ancient type, the ones in which
You really appear as you, your other self,
Yearning for release, for being-seen,
And the soul, divided, behind it,
Yearning too for unity. Oh my divided
Soul, walk with me this night along
The narrow streets and allies, among
The ordinary houses with their one lamp
Or a porch light on, and witness,
As if suspended in a lucid trance, the pale
Translucence of reflection: mirrors
Through which you can move your hands,
Mirrors like water, though an airy medium,
In which the prophecy of fulfillment
Changes constantly: if only you could
Pull your being back from that strange,
Luminous darkness, as you see your eyes
Burning with desire at strange angles,
Like the faces of the people in a small plane
Doing aerobatics. And sometimes
Not just your eyes, but eyes you have loved,
Or love now, eyes you yearn for as much
As you yearn for your own soul, though
No one but me accompanies you now:
They, too, are calling you to arms.
Yet what can you do but walk among them,
Like a beekeeper to his swarm, softly
Calling and calling their names?
Small consolation they may hear,
Or sense, your tending, if they nevertheless
Turn, and return, to their small hexagons.

BRING YOUR NIGHTS WITH YOU

TO THE HARBORMASTER

In Memory of Frank O'Hara

Among those I loved you were the first.
From my sixth week I knew that you
Were everywhere, dwelling in the oldest
Sycamores and scrub pines at the mainland's
Edge, when it is dark and the foxes have crept
Among their branches, dwelling as well
At the center where the fishing boats haul
Their daily flounder, bass, crab, lobster,
And the waterskiers fill their Evinrude tanks.
Sundays I prayed to God. Other days I watched
As you clanged the swing bridge open and shut
For the sailboats and the Coast Guard cutter,
Laying its fine swath, its deck guns and its lifeboats,
On a sharp line up and down Townsend's Inlet
And out to sea. You hauled the broken-down
And injured back to shore, you sought and hailed
The stranded on the innumerable islands
That were, in some strange abstraction, all
Seven Mile Island. Only once did I call,
So stranded, and you did not come.
I was older then. I never knew you,
But until I left, I knew you held the harbor
In your capacious hand, though it was never
A hand I touched. It may be that your reasonings
Were, like the islands, abstracted as only one reasoning,
Eternal, but of that kind whose only choice
Was to prevent my ever reaching you.

A SHADOW ON THE MOON

I know: a fallacy, to claim you most belong to us
In darkness, as if the shadow that we cast
Across your seas and highlands bound you
That much more—light, and loss of light
The key, not gravitation. I have lost much
Light here. Thus my interest in your unseen
Presence, among the many versions of the loved
And lovers following my orbit, some long dead,
Some not yet met, and each distinct and imperceptible
As you. We draw to us we know not who: they go
In and out of the darkness as they must, though we
Deduce their presence from known facts. That other
Immaterial deduction shadows every waking day,
However, and in sleep I dream of you as if
Our earthly home did not exist, and you
Returned and turned again across the sun
As luminous as you have always been,
Not needing us nor conscious of a loss,
Bright vision of the lives I gave away.

DARK WING

Pitch. Turn. Roll. Three axes
In the light or dark of the moon.

Terms. Words. Words approximating
A condition, a position in space.

You were waiting for advice?
Trim. Wings level. For this the ailerons

And horizontal stabilizer may suffice.
Aft, that device creates a downward force

The wings combat with lift. By contrast,
Forward, a canard, that tiny piece

Of history from France in 1906.
It produces continuous lift,

Something of a miracle for a body in
Space. Even now, when a canard wing

Flies over, we look up, so unusual, unlikely,
So like us. It comes with a high coefficient

Of instability. It tends toward the deep stall.
Yet, respected, loved even, it does all

That was ever asked of a wing—on,
And on, and then more, heedless of the sun.

AFTER DRINKING ALL NIGHT WITH A FRIEND, I GO OUT
IN A BOAT AT DAWN
TO SEE WHO CAN WRITE THE BEST POEM

For Robert Bly

Someone is missing. . .Ah, now I see you there, waving
On the shore, not drowning. I overlooked something,
And you are dead, and this moment in which I am sailing
Is fifty years separate from your moment, with your friend,

The failure, whoever he was. You two, of course,
Were in a rowboat, not being quite capable of handling more.
My tack is sure. I've cleated the sheets cleanly; the sails
Snap near Grand Marais, Superior, which is dark,

Not pale, fed over and over by cool springs. It wells beneath me
The way air wells up under a wing, the way the low pressure
Of the air lifts, as it lifts the outward edge of these sails,
Drawing them forward into a day and a heading

You have already traveled, still somewhere beyond
My experience. But I am getting there, my friend.
This morning I write to say: Yes. You won.
But I am on course. And, Robert, not far behind.

THE FIRST NIGHT

There was never a question—no dream.
Nor was the voice inside my head, an incipient
Sign of schizophrenia, at which no one would have been

Surprised. No: in the darkness of the far room, *la voz*
Comenzó: "There they are. The soft eyes open. I listen. If they
have lived in a wood, it is a wood. If they have lived
on plains it is grass rolling under their feet forever.

And I was about to speak, or at least to say:
"James Dickey, a poem no one remembers now,"
But she was unquestionably "she," though not to touch,

Not *there*—not, to be fair, the lover I had craved
For years. A small laugh. Then: *Being, whose flesh*
Dissolves at our touch, knower of the secret sums and measures,

You are always here. Imagine the best part of yourself
Turned outward, the ultimate narcissism becoming
Another reality, and speaking back to you in the words

You memorized, from others, in a voice not yours.
I sleep next to books and nautical charts: the last time
A body tangled herself with mine was in late May, 2015.

Thus it should be the ultimate loneliness, that disembodied voice.
She said: *At the cycle's center they tremble, they walk under the tree,*
They fall, they are torn, they rise, they walk again. I was given

The memory of the farmhouse at Fruitlands, the docent,
The bed she bounced up and down on a little, Louisa May
Alcott's bed, my sad wife, our two-year-old son. That is how

I understood. *Any body can die.* We all lose the one we lie
Closest to, the one whose flesh brings us to sleep.
This was the after, only it was now, only it was not.

The italicized quotations are from Antonio Machado's "Los Sueños
Dialogados," James Dickey's "The Heaven of Animals," Wendell Berry's "To
the Unseeable Animal," and Robert Pinsky's "ABC."

POEM FOR MY BIRTHDAY, JUNE 11TH, 2011

They can't see, so they need to be trained in improvisation.
A.L. Kennedy, "Confectioner's Gold"

Of course it looks real. And the old conundrum
About appearance as illusion is exactly that.
Something is there. The problem is, it's not

That something, but some other thing, something
We can't appropriate. We can never see it. It is the cardinal
That is not the cardinal, the wild rose that is not

A lilac but also not a rose—that instinct we have
That makes us talk, still, about the soul, or spirit,
Which we know we cannot see. Infuriating, yes,

That it should ever have been a comfort. This
Is our limit and antagonist, this blindness.
The soul is what we say it is. So is the spirit.

We make them up, and the house lights go down,
And we are solo on the stage, a world breathless
With anticipation. Or not. Perhaps no one cares.

Still, that moment of knowing you are completely
On your own, in the dark, in the stage light, that
What comes out of your mouth will absolutely

Define you, finally—finally, the relief. Even if
You are completely wrong, in some way, you have made
The avatar, the thing unlike the seen and yearning,

Not to be known, nor ever to be witnessed, but merely
Performed the way a serious Shakespearean might do it,
As if, between stage left and right, there were one true story.

SPARE POEM

What to keep in reserve. . .
During the Cuban Missile Crisis
My parents filled the basement
With canned chili, peas, beans,

Water, cling peaches, Cheerios,
Peanut butter and powdered milk,
About the time Anne Sexton
Was writing "innumerable goods."

We never touched it, I don't think.
Bad memories, bad karma.
But always there, in reserve.
All my life, what I've learned

Is to stockpile for disaster,
Then keep bad memories,
Bad karma, in masterly reserve.
Just in case. In case of what?

Something good getting the upper
Hand? If I had a cellar of canned goods
I'd break them out on my birthday.
It would be the anti-Last Supper.

"Take and eat: this is my bad karma,
The flesh and blood of my bad memories."
We would party like the Dharma Bums,
And everything would be gone,

Including the dreadful peaches.
That night, even if I were alone,
Would be my first dreamless sleep,
The sleep of the dead destined to return.

IN THE ASCENDANT

In the ascendant darkness
Let there be no minor happenstance
Or fear of accident. Here

Intention is everything—thus
The fluster of lost door keys
Faint cries in the alleys of terror,

Luxuriant trauma held inside
Someone's unknowing carelessness.
On the other hand, among the soft

And layered petals of the night,
The nightshade opening to its
Sweet fullness, the only response

Is *I mean this*—how could you not?
The dark and not the light set you
In motion. Alone, and yet engaged

With the sensuous unseen, you hear
A phrase from childhood as if anew:
"I move at the heart of the world."

ANTICIPATION

The air here is sultry with tomorrow's heat.
I move around the house, touching the white-

Hot passion of the furniture—this couch, this chair,
This tiled floor, bannister, this carpeted stair,

This doorway, sheets, down comforter, this bed.
It is more than possible to live in the future. Instead

Of waiting here, tending to errands and distracting
Myself, I concentrate all feeling on the resurrecting

Drama of tomorrow, encased in the unreality of now
Until, alive in the unreality, I find the power to allow

The touch that, not yet here, has even so transformed
This present to a fiction I can finally understand.

FOR A YOUNG CHILD WHO PUT
A FLASHLIGHT IN THE FREEZER

I don't know if you expected me to find it or not.
I tried to think when you had done it, but you
Are always hiding things—car keys. Leftovers.
Once I needed two weeks to find my glasses.
I still haven't found the Kawasaki Ninja key.
So this might be the game you play to win.
At first that's what I thought. Later, after the flashlight
Thawed, I realized you'd left it on—the cold
Gradually had shut down the chemical reaction
Of the batteries. At room temperature they re-ignited,
Albeit dimly. It seems you wanted light
In a dark place, even if no one could see it,
Even if only you knew it was there. Secret light
In a dark place—who doesn't want that, really,
Although rarely does it get so literal. At almost three,
However, you are in some different category
Literal, like the cupcake crumbs you leave
Between the cushions of the couch, intentionally,
But more than literal, as you enjoy my furious
Eradication of the ants. How funny grown-ups
Must seem to you. And yet you prove what you
Most wish, I think, to unprove: our worlds
Do not conjoin. What you do excludes me,
Though sometimes you bewail the confusion.
Each night, more and more, I think: I do not
Belong in your world, nor you in mine.
Most parents, I think, think this sometimes.
But not so ardently. And you seek that edge,
That gap. Where the light is, in the dark,
Is where no grownup is, or child—only
You, or rather me, whoever you are,
I am, leaving clues to solo mysteries.

THE HISTORY OF REST

No one knows. In the midst of it
One tends to forget what it is,
Or really that any other state
Could exist: "rest in peace"
Is nonsensical, as if one could really
Rest in agitation or perpetual surprise.
I want to say: *This is how rest began.*
And of course we all know the story
Of the seventh day, but what, exactly,
Is that story? We honor it, to the extent
We do, by going to church or synagogue,
But those have their separate days and litanies.
They are not the divine narrative of rest. It was
Evening and it was morning, so time passed,
But the connotation is of strenuous
Exertion and its aftermath. How like us
To know in great detail the nature
Of exertion but to have no language
For its complement. Am I at rest, now,
Writing this? Foolish question. Today,
On NPR, the town of Empire, Nevada
Was shut down, a Gypsum company town.
The man whose job it was to close the town
Mentioned, in passing, that yes, it was fun
To go to Reno for a meal or for groceries,
But sometimes he just drove into the desert
Where, he said, you could climb a mountain
And be the only person for 400 square miles.
I liked that man, despite his job. He understood
Some things that, in the end, have no known end.

GRACE

In the world before grace, the dawn
Kept its council in the first run of time
When the animals, extinct and present,
Slept—trilobite, small rodent, great cat,
Mammoth—alert to the enormous change
Unknowing that the world, past its old
Darkness, turning yet unmoved, would bring.

After grace, the world turned in the years' span
Of loss and bliss, unmoored from day or night,
Where the leopard and the wild dog and woman
And man as well among them lay down in sorrow
Without cause and then rose up, among the living
And the dead, dizzyingly spun in the wide vales
Of wonder, in diurnal surges toward the sun.

NIGHT RIDE HOME

The mister who knew which way is home
Having departed long ago, as Anne foretold,
His routes are now the long, unrolling lanes
Delivering forlorn history between the darker
Corn and soybeans filling out the contours
Of the night, with a stray car or pickup
Straggling from a bar or domestic tragedy—
And a lone rider, having committed
"On the Move" to memory from childhood
And "Music Swims Back to Me" only
A little later, faster and faster, till the turns
Tighten down and he leans into a centrifugal
Force with a lean identical to flying,
His ties to the road as tenuous as his ties
To the abandoned route to home, which
God knows he may even now be in the act
Of finding and losing because of some new veracity
About some old thing he did not know he wanted,
All the time, which was escape velocity.

WHAT THEY FOUND UNDER THE STRAW
IN A STALL OF THE ABANDONED BARN

Christmas Eve day and nothing to do. They pulled on
Bib overalls, boots, and gloves and coats, and went exploring
Down the unplowed road. The old house had been boarded up

For years, tight as a shamanic drum. No point in even trying.
But the barn, as such things go, had been left to rot: the back
Hay loft already collapsed onto the stalls, the worry that even

Pulling back one of the doors would cause the rest to fall.
But they were young and didn't care. Who were "they"? Don't
Ask. "Let's look there," one said, and so they went to the second

Stall on the left, just next to what had fallen in, the most dangerous.
They kicked the straw around. "Nothing," one said, but then
Someone said "Wait," and so they knelt and pushed the straw

More carefully. What they found must once have been a book—
The leather covers, rotted now, and most of the pages gone.
Someone's hand-written story on the rest. There had been

A child. . .What had happened? The only other remnant page
Was a shaft of light, not yellow, but white on white, acrylic
On Strathmore: head-on you couldn't see it, but tilt it toward

The winter sun and it was blinding. They looked around some more.
That small pile of straw in the corner. Underneath, the edge
Of a white sheet with some blood, and as they pulled, more

White sheets bundled, more blood, and a clump of something
Reeking of itself, of death. They ran. They never told anyone.
How did I hear of it? I was one of them. I came to know what we

Had found when I first read *the uncontrollable mystery on the bestial floor.*

THE FORMALISTS

The land is filled with cries of disorder.
Against them stand, in this time as before,

The ones who measured to the world its solitude
In numbered syllables and weight sufficient to elude

The sharpest principles of chaos. Like statuary
Of dark metal, thronged around with mastery

Of violence, they linger where they are brought:
Even if, for a time, cries fade, though the sight

Defies credulity, contorted bodies in their avenues
Of blood, the formal casts its shadow on the news

That is always news: these words survive,
Though no one says them. Order makes them live

In a universe that, in the end, does not require ours
Though they are born here. Wherever they are, theirs

Is a world apart, a bronze-cast palm beyond the last thought,
Bronze cast of words past reason, for which no one fought.

THE REVELATION

The revelation is not distant,
Nor is it at hand. It is a Joseph
Cornell box with little shelves
Filled with Barnett Newmans.
It lives in drains and unbuilt lots,
Continuous distractions, Season Five
of *Weeds,* whatever moves you.
It is the thing you criticize.
It is what you hate most
About yourself. It lies
At the heart of the lover
You drive away. You can tell
Where it has been: there is
A residue, not of regret,
Or even grief at loss,
But of something enormous,
Sensuous, and kind, misunderstood.
Angry. Punitive. Surging and failing
Into forgiveness, indifference even.
It haunts people, places—glass shards
At City Recycling, the ones that cut
When you try to do a good deed,
Picking them up. You knew
It would have to be this way.
You make things to defend yourself.

CHRISTMAS NOTE TO SELF

The things that mattered, didn't—cars, jobs—
Why be more than generic?—even bill collectors:
They came and went. Love came and went, too,

Like water over a small dam our children made
One summer simply to watch the thrill of water
Falling, of being able to do that—but no: never

Generic. We are close, here, to a hope that is true
For some and false for others, and we might
Enumerate reasons, but like love itself those

Reasons would be lost in the falling water. Visitations
From the dead, Louisa May Alcott out of nowhere
And very different from all of her biographies,

Biographers, not "that girl"—back to acquire
The lusts that life denied her, back to converse
About the nature of unselfconscious being, what we

Call "death." And the others—always, in shamanic
Practice in the Upper World, the most difficult
And dangerous, the man in the long white gown

And the eagle who swoops down and low overhead,
Then spirals up and up till he lands atop the mountain
Just beside the man—the two looking down with obvious

Sorrow: This was not what was to have been, this narrative.
The denizens of the Upper World cannot prevent mistakes
Here. They can offer promises, amend elsewhere the aberrations.

UNREAL CITY

It is possible to imagine almost anything,
Though William James believes it is impossible
To imagine one's own death. This seems to me,
By contrast, the simplest task, with practice:

One goes about the room, looking at the door,
The shelves, the books, the TV, dresser, changing table,
Toys and memorabilia, and one by one erases each
From thought. It is an exercise, yes, and requires

Repetition, but in the end is simply one more skill,
Perhaps the best. For the ambitious, shift the scale:
Central Park, say, on the day before Thanksgiving.
You have come here on a holiday but you have

No money. Enough for a subway back to Brooklyn.
Nothing for a sandwich, a snack, much less a meal.
The well-dressed and their children swirl around you
Like leaves, playing and laughing. The leaves

Play and laugh. Then, instead of feeling desperate,
You erase: Happy people. Children. Leaves. Antique trees.
Pond. Plaza Hotel. Dakotas. The woman you are with.
Yourself. Incredibly, the not-you is not non-being,

Nor is it aphasic, but it is listening to and feeling
The something that is there when nothing else is.
It calls you with the sound of wind in autumn.
It is one place, perhaps the one place, you belong.

THE SECRET PLACE OF THE MOST HIGH

January 3, 2012

In grief, invariably I seek refuge
In my father's habits: I work on the car.
At 208,308 miles, this Subaru has far
Surpassed a common life expectancy. But what

Is that, really, that phrase—as if it meant something:
"Life expectancy." My son's great-grandmother
Would have been 86 three days from now.
She died on New Year's Day. My mother

Died at 60. Just before, the number three cylinder
On my father's VW Beetle lost compression. After
They lowered my mother into the earth, my father
Got a winch and lifted the engine clean out of the car.

Today I did a little thing, change the oil,
Though with a wind chill of zero it was no
Small labour, and I kept mixing up clockwise-
Counterclockwise. Always something.

My father survived a couple of months,
Reboring the cylinder, replacing the piston
And rings, putting it all back together.
New life expectancy. Then he went over

The edge, and never returned. His demise
Took a long, long time: for all the times death
Is unkind, it was life, then, that killed him daily.
I see him still, standing by the engine

As by an altar: of course we would be above
Reproach if we married only what we could
Replenish, or assist, or set right—instead we do
The opposite because of love. Of love. Love.

COMING ABOUT

If the body of water is large enough,
An inlet, say, or even something crazier,
A half-mile out to sea, you can stow
The oars and lie in the boat as it dips
And spins, slowly, coming about again
And again, though the peaks and troughs
May swamp you if you're not alert,
And of course you're not alert,
Just lying there. It's a crapshoot.
It's not "a path with heart."
But you have to choose to let go.

If I said, "The past is like that,"
You would have to hunt with annoyance
For too-ingenious hidden meaning. But,
Though the past is like that, I was really
Thinking of its alternative, coming about
Again and again in a sailboat, pushing
The tiller to leeward, the hull wallowing
And waves sloshing over the side
As the sail luffs for a moment,
Then catches, and you cleat the sheet
Smartly. Normally you would be tacking

Into the wind to get somewhere—
Home would be the obvious choice,
But in any case a destination—safe
In the harbor. Why do it over and over
In the ocean where nobody is, and no one
Can help? Let's say you don't need help,
You're tired of destinations, arrivals
Being even worse than departures,
And you know that this is risky,
Even pointless. Yet each tack brings you
Closer to capsize, which is why you smile.

UNSTOPPABLE

Not anxiety, but rather curiosity makes me wonder:
When will the words stop? How funny,
To have made a life among them,
When they are not even, strictly speaking,
Necessary: my weakness, a kind
Of secondary passion, is neurology,
In which we learn that words are thrice
Removed, in neural patterning,
From anything the body knows.
If we truly loved the truth of being,
We would communicate only in images
And music. So all these words are evidence
I hate the truth of my own being? No. . .
I hear the counter-argument, that words
Reveal to us the long way back to the *nous*:
What would Plotinus be without the *Enneads*?
Yet much of that appears unnecessary,
And dear Aquinas said, on his deathbed,
After the *Summa Theologica* and the *Summa
Contra Gentiles,* that all his words "seemed
As straw" compared to what he'd seen.
What he'd seen. . .Let us say there is a truth
Of being, at any given second, and it leaves
A trail, like a quark, in language. Physicist
Of the soul, trapped and freed by exactly
This life history, I will write the almost unobservable,
That one day it will be the story of how and where
I passed through, at an almost-inconceivable speed.

SADNESS, ITS NATURAL HISTORY

It has a natural history. Why should one
Not be sad? The day is full of sun.
It is warm. You can walk and say

To yourself, "no past," but it changes nothing.
Why are you alone? If out of cruel
Necessity you ranked your loves,

Which was the worst loss? Was it all
Your fault, or can you say? Everyone
Of them is happy now, as far as you can tell,

Although sometimes they, too, must be
Sad. At birth we were parted from the thing
We fear in death. In between, the flashes

Of genius—the great poems of imperfection,
The brilliant harmonies, the sub-atomic
Particles—are flashes of return. In mind

They feel like love. We love what we most
Fear, and dread admitting it. No wonder
When the sun is insufficient comfort.

PRIVACY

I came to the town square
When the moon hung full
In the daytime sky, but you
Were not there. It was my
Mistake: you had never actually said
You would be. At the playground,
Children chased and screamed,
Swung up and down or climbed,
Tentatively, the places that were
Mostly empty space. Timing
Is not merely everything,
It is also private: on a jungle gym
A certain three-year-old can do
Things a seven-year-old will not,
Cannot. We could never talk
All the way down to our privacies:
We told stories instead, which look
Intimate but deceive us. Stories
Are the cenotaphs of privacy.
Now we speak to each other
In measures of music almost
Entirely resistant to denotation,
Grazing those secret places
Finally, though we may never
See one another again.

THE POEM OF FURTHEST MEMORY

It is like nothing at all, yet perfect
As a miniature, perhaps from this
Far perspective—it is a thing only,
An amulet. Rotate it—an American
Urn: little streets and houses and cars,
A beach, girl friend new suddenly
In a bathing suit. Everything is in place.
It was the way things, once set
In motion, turned out exactly
As they should, not as they did.
I must admit that it is beautiful.
It has nothing to do with me.

OH MY HEART

Oh my heart, if there had been another choice
I would have made that choice. I will never
Know now if I betrayed you, or if it was
The other way around, you sly and furtive.

All the syllables of yearning now are out
Of order, or I hear them as if they were
The Latin I was supposed to learn
Many years ago, but did not—the book

Is still on the shelf with its 35-year-old
Note from my lover: "You have other
Work to do!" The notecard has faded
From orange to white. Incomprehensible,

This yearning that once made sense. Or did it?
Last night I dreamed I lived in a small,
Rented room, single bed and hot plate,
And suddenly a woman beckoned me

To a mansion where everyone I had ever loved
Had gathered, so relieved to see me. Does that
Make sense? Today I am alone with you, my
Heart, and no solitude to keep us company.

INTERLUDE: AUBADE

When you are gone, with someone less like you
Though more your age, I will return then to this page
To see the prophecy I wrote so long before. This stage was,
After all, my first home. Thus I must be true
To origins, the one way I can still be true to you.
We met in song, the Lennon lines between us
Suited to two older types, two working-class
Performers well along, and looking back—
But, singing, we were looking down a track
Whose final station was impossible to view.
And, yes, sometimes I thought that tunnel light
Was not the resurrection, but a train in sight.
I still think, sometimes, think we may be right
And the world wrong, however great the cost.
If that is true, regardless, you and I will not be lost.

THIS POEM, MY HAND, THE BOOK

We do not live paper lives. And yet
Those lives survive us, revising us.

This poem, for example, about devotion.
"Cut loose, without devotion, a man

Becomes a comic"—my hand in the iPhone
Photo of the poem, holding it flat so that it grows

Into the fullness of its being. There is a limit
In the poem to what the man can do. His body,

Excellent dog that it is, comes to his rescue.
Out of the work of rescue comes, ironically,

Not the word on paper, but the image
Of the hand—tan, with sinuous fingers,

Crippled where a storm window guillotined
The thumb fifteen years ago. The hand,

Its wound, its tenderness, direct extension
Of the heart. My hand, to you, however

You can accept it. The book comes,
Not from the page, but from all the implicit

Motions of the hand as it seeks to open,
Hold, and half-release what it most cherishes.

That is the work of hands, the immaculate story,
The motion toward the life still lived in private,

No matter how large and brilliant the book,
No matter how infinitesimal the poem.

THINGS I REMEMBER

When taking off in a float plane, ignore the sinking feeling
At the rear as the pontoons dig in: when speed comes
And you feel yourself suddenly hovering, never forget
You are still in the water. First lift the upwind pontoon,
Then the downwind one—if you try to pull both up at once
You'll never get into the air. When landing, carry some power
Right down to the water—no power-off landings. In general,
Come about into the wind, but if you absolutely have to jibe,
Release the tension on the traveler so you don't capsize.
When all else fails, furl the mainsail and most of the jib,
Throw out the sea anchor, and batten down the hatches.
Strap yourself into the bunk, but prepare for sudden exit,
Even upside down, and have the raft at the ready. Life jackets
Are your call—some would rather drown quickly in a storm,
Others have it in them to expect a rescue. When climbing
A tree, always imagine yourself as something else—a pilot
Ascending or descending, a mountain-climber, a hawk
Choosing a resting place or a meal. It will change the way
You move, change your balance, make you lithe and agile.
And if you fall, you will catch a branch before you crash.
If you are a two-year-old and your parents tell you to go
Get your own milk, drag a chair to the kitchen light switch,
Never a stool. You will save your front teeth that way.
If, in your crib, a cat jumps in while you are crying
And lays itself across your face, there is nothing you can do.
It is the first lesson. If you survive, later, you remember.

THE NAMES OF THE LOST

"In 'In This Valley' Amichai sees/searches for a valley home where you can start afresh without dying and you can love without forgetting the other love. Did he find this valley? I have not."—anonymous Post-It *in a library copy of Nili Gold's biography of Yehuda Amichai.*

Proximity to overwhelming, completely unforeseen happiness
Paradoxically makes us prone to hear loss more sharply—

Not just that there is so much of it, or that, in the end,
We lose everything, but rather the strangeness of it

As a kind of subtext to daily life: passing minutes, lines
At the bank, lines of poetry that will end, dull classes,

Debt, mortgages, accidents, trials—it might remind us
Of kindergarten, or first grade, when the enormity

Of what we will later call the Social Apparatus
Began to dawn on us, and we wanted to flee

Or just do Before and After School—anything not to enter
The world of the lost. Headlines today: 1.8 million

African American men are somehow "unaccounted for"
In the United States. The accountant of Auschwitz

Goes on trial. Poor migrant deaths in the Mediterranean
May hit 30,000 this year. Of course Amichai would seek

A continuous world, without loss. It would have to be
In that valley that a home, and love, would become real.

But amoral love defies even the unnamed names of the lost,
Blowing from the northwest with a scent not spring-like

But salty, refusing the backward glance. And we must look back
Anyway, spreading our sails because there is nothing else to spread.

WAITING

Wolves howl; the forest, on the edge of space,
Splays out its dangers. I pace around the room,
Where walls create that space, and everywhere
Is terror or exhaustion. A tame dog, framed in the raw
Deal of time, may pace itself to sleep, teetering
Into a dog-dream. Half-wild still, more like the wolves
I fear, I yearn for them. But if I stopped and turned,
Would they remember me, my scent? Could I
Return? Or would they do what all wolves do?

WHATEVER IT IS

Whatever it is, it isn't about ships, or moorings.
It isn't really about dreams, though dreams are there.
It's about the unnamable we would do anything to name,
Because to name it would contain it, bring it under control.

It can't be done. Al Alvarez, speaking of Plath: the unnamable
"Seized her by the throat and shook her." And she wrote
The *Ariel* poems, and her death was more witness
To the way she couldn't stand the strain, the not-naming.

But earlier, at the outset, were the three postcards—
Two from Ted to her, one from her to him. Diane Middlebrook
Describes it as a kind of range-finding: Who are you?
Where are you? Can you hear me? The terrible shock

Of the answer, in a sudden clearing: I hear you.
I am here. The scarcely-being-able-to-breath.
Small, greedy beings, we want it all Right Now,
Want everything answered, every wound dressed,

And all the unknown known. But whatever it is
Lives and moves and has its being in the unknown,
And it brings us to its lair when we're not looking.
Should we then continue to believe it means us well?

BLACK DRESS JEAN JACKET

Luck comes in runs. You know it best when it's bad.
Good luck starts to feel like the way life should be,

Until it's not. Still, there's the matter of style:
You can prep for the bad with savings, or a tight

Circle of friends, or an exit strategy—a long,
Long road trip, heroin, "the solace of open spaces"—

But on the whole it's better to have something
In the closet—one thing, or two, to make it count:

Black dress jean jacket. It's never not a statement.
You walk in, and everyone knows. You're not

Afraid of death, and if you're grieving, the heart
Beneath your sleeve is the heart beneath denim.

Don't mess with it. It's been out on the town before,
A lot, and it knows everything there is to know

About bad luck. Good luck. Style. It took awhile
To find this particular jacket. Not every jean jacket

Suits a funeral. And the black dress, well,
you could get married in it. Who says white

Is luck? Who cares about the illusion of virginity?
None of us is virgin—bad luck happens at birth.

Some of us learn protection better than others.
Some of us make it a style. A statement. The future.

COLD

There comes a time when we must stop
With the mind of winter. The cold is for us to feel—
Chill in the recesses of the chest, and painful breath,
The incipient agony of frostbite in the hands. This
Is pain we cannot think. It is pain. Because ours is
An embodied life. We forget—we think we can think
It through. When first the world touches the body,
The body becomes the world, living each day
In its way to the edge of risk. Each day the unthinkable
Becomes more and more the body's whole being,
Its core determination—to feel the field as the field
Goes fallow, to feel the stalk wither, the grass curl
Under new snow. Miraculous, that touch I remember:
When, ever before, did my body make such sense?
But making sense to me is not the point. My body
Saw its likeness and accepted the similitude with what
The body would call gratitude if the body spoke.
The body does not speak. The body knows.

DEPRESSION SPEAKS ON THE EVE
OF ITS TWENTIETH ANNIVERSARY

I have outlasted everyone. I outlasted your wife
And seven lovers. You think you drove them away,
That you are unlovable? I drove them away.
You do yourself too much credit, thinking that
At heart you are awful and cruel. I am the genius
Of cruelty. I have injured you with slow, enormous,
Even bureaucratic precision, so that, after 21
Different anti-depressants and one hospitalization,
You scramble every day for the pretense of functional.
At your best moments, now, you are anesthetized
With alcohol, one of my dearest allies. True, I have not,
To my great disappointment, found a way
To vanquish you. And there is that other risk
I always weigh: if you die, I die. But right now
You will do almost anything to make me stop.
Even now, from the tiniest distance, I watch you plan
A life change you believe would vanquish me.
I doubt myself. That is my one weakness.
If you do what you are thinking, I feel
In my own narrowing dark hours, you may
Undo the work I take to be my great accomplishment.
True, it would not happen all at once. But I feel
The tremors. Yes, you are worrying me.
Yes, I should not tell you this. This is a love letter
From a burning building. Don't you love me
For my devotion? Think: Don't you love *me*?
For the first time now in twenty years, you frighten me.

AND THEN YOU

If a tree
                falls   in the forest

        he ducks and   flinches

                thinking defense,   too many

beatings and the   Zapruder film

            over   and   over

while   from   the corner

        of his left eye   he   catches her,

                curious,   unalarmed.

The week before,

        full lunar eclipse,   he texts her   about how

            we learn
superstition.

                Looking up,   she sees   a sign.

Now   she says   "A tree fell in the forest

        just for us."   Hours later

still he is shocked   at her sure wonder,

            like a mist   rising up

                from the face of the moon.

LIKE KITTENS

"Vardaman, the youngest child, is traumatized horribly by his mother's death, and continues to confuse her with the fish he caught and killed earlier that same day."

This one is mostly black—hardly any brown or orange.
It had a late start in the spring, though the winter past

Was mild—it pauses at your feet as we align
Along the earthen dam. You kneel down. I kneel.

If this is benediction, it is anxious—the wooly
Caterpillar slowly dithers, evading your open palm

I would accept. You gather it, gently, with your other
Hand. Finally in your palm, it moves like a tiny kitten—

Say ten days old—as it searches for a teat, or warmth,
Or something new that it can sense but not yet see.

This most entrances me—this, and the quiet,
And its blackness against your pale skin, and your

Tattoo—"My mother is a fish"—whose significance
Hits home so suddenly that I forget the words

I utter—"Like tiny kittens!"—and you will have
To remind me later. What should this, the larval

Stage of *Pyrrharctia isabella,* The Isabella tiger moth,
Have to do with the 25 births of kittens I witnessed

As a child? Perhaps we make too much of species:
This one prefers your skin to your shirt, and moves

Inquisitively from your hand to mine and back.
I can think of other intimacies, but none more intimate:

The three of us, in this sun-drenched, ordinary place,
Belong here. I didn't know till now. I didn't know.

NAVY

The moment before lights out, immeasurable night,
Dark matter blazing all that we are not, and also
Joint forces, ships at sea where you have never been

And what lies below, full fathom five before
The world of whales and submarines. I grew up
In your medium: from the age of six I always had

A Navy pea coat for winter, heavy wool that sailors
Wore on deck, impervious to wind and rain but a risk
If someone called "Man overboard." I never did.

Funny that the Navy should indulge in puns: the hue
Was always luminous, profound. It welcomed secrets,
Held them close and safe. And in it, in the black of winter,

I would dream of summer, and the boats of Avalon,
The Sunfish and the Dyer Dhow, earliest inscriptions
Of my freedom. I could go anywhere, even out to sea

Through Townsends Inlet, though in an eight-foot boat
No one would call that safe. I did it. I would do it now.
No matter. What matters is the texture, color, and the

Ritual lovingkindness of the wool, the cut, the fit,
The weight, the life scarcely to be imagined finally real
In the folds of the garment. Navy was my first home,

Flight instructor father and an artist-mother, palettes
Strewn around the house and my favorite colour always
Arresting in its ritual phrase: "I am here because of you."

BRING YOUR NIGHTS WITH YOU

Quoting W.S. Merwin

I was not looking for happiness
Quiet and jagged

I wanted to be seen

You came with your night goggles
Not quite an officer from a foreign war

In the light we share
The voluptuousness of looking

In the night we share
Whatever can be seen of us

In the end
It is not the hour

Forever or
Already gone

What matters
Is the standing-out

Among the celebrants
The singularity—
You and I our injured bodies

Eyes darting
Contagious fire
Contagious silences

The navy before the violet

Semaphore of color
Signaling that annunciation
That mutual retreat

LANDSCAPE

Here the valleys run parallel, dozens, hundreds.
You can't see them all if you fly over, because
You can't fly high: clouds obscure them all.

Rain. Sometimes quiet, sometimes like hard words.
Quiet rain is peace. Hard words are what we train for.
While we live we are immortal in the rain, although

Each valley has its cemetery. It is all compromise:
The trees are mended, though the stones are broken.
The trains run north-south, mile to unknown mile—

We laid the track, but no one ever measured. We just
Laid rail until we reached the end, and then we turned
And laid the rail back. Tired as we are of gentle gloom,

We take the trains, which charge no fare in any valley.
Few trains are express. Most stop irregularly—there is no
Master board at any station, just the names on platforms.

The trains wait. In all these valleys, all these years,
No one has ever lain across the tracks, no train has ever
Found a tractor-trailer stuck and hit the morning news.

I have been to every valley, walking alongside the rails
In my old Gore-Tex, riding sometimes—a few times
Taking necessary tests, becoming driver, engineer.

My train. But at one terminus I set out, the way I once did,
Pack and freeze-dried food and tent, and climbed the end
Where all the valleys terminate. I can tell you, rumours

Are true: my head just grazing the grey clouds, I saw
The perpendicular valley. In myth it was named,
But the name was wrong. No train. No rain except

As needed. Sun. The blessed sun I read about in books.
The books had had it right. All this time we lived in text,
And here was an end. Why? So I could bring this back to you.

GARDEN PARTY

In the end, everyone left. I understood. But just before,
In the tiny garden behind the house, I threw a private party.
The guests were the you who knew me, or who might
Have known me, just after that moment of affirmation
Or refusal, and those same versions of me, the ultimate
Narcissist apparently, but no—not exactly—the question
Derives from a much-contested set of equations: does what
We call "reality" branch off from the trunk line, each time
We fuck someone or even just say "hi" at Hy-Vee,
The trunk line and the lifetime of branches all happening
Simultaneously somewhere, or does the trunk line vanish,
And the branch without its root become reality at the instant
It is also simulacrum? The latter is clever but irritating
In the way, at least to me, it affirms Occam's Razor,
Which I myself believe in practice but not in theory:
And now, or just before, is exactly the time for theory.
Thus I send out two dozen invitations—one dozen
To myself, and the other to, well, those others in probability:
RSVP. No one replies. But at the appointed time, when I
Bring the crudités and drinks out to the small tables, there
You all are. We are. But there is a cost for such hubris:
None of you, or us, see me, though I am there, and when
A couple of times initially I try to interrupt I quickly
Grasp the futility. I would go on with a faint shimmer
Of the might-have-been, asking, "Do I know you?"
Over and over, and everyone would say, "Yes," and I
Would scrunch up my translucent face and laugh a little.
No memory even of this, though I am telling this to you.

CHELSEA HOTEL NUMBER

All I could think of was "I am ugly but we have the music"   but you were

looking out the window at the Bayou Contraband   feeding   into Indian Bay and I had heard you say "I need you I don't need you." And I had

told you I thought that was true   although I told you something else as well. This was a deviation from the trip,   Lake Charles.   Below us people were gambling. Above us, gambling. Here people gambled on the roof   and you could

throw your failed self off and instead of falling   you   would actually float upward, as appears to be happening in Jonathan Safran Foer's *Extremely Loud and Incredibly Close*   if you follow the normal narrative structure   from left to right, beginning to end but when did we ever do that?   Earlier

you conjured a spell where the embryo   of   all   male   desire spilled from your body   as well as the tongues of the Pentecost sliced in their viscous blood   from the hatred against them   and the host   of   the   Holy   Ghost,   damp   with   labial   thrill   unarrested   and the first prayer book you ever received   some mother shoved up there a long time ago.

You didn't do this to shock me.   You did this   because   you needed a witness   someone   who   told   stories   backward   or sideways who behaved old-fashioned.   Downstairs   the limousines wait for the unfallen.   Downstairs your heart will be a legend but not yet   but here   this is where I confess   my promise not to lie to you   oppressed as we are   by the figures of beauty from entirely

different though not dissimilar sources and you told me   what you told me   after you unclenched your fist   after   you   turned your back on the crowd.

GRANITE

"The Circular Ruins" is a short story by Jorge Luis Borges

It began, as these things do, with the imagining of extreme heat
Until the imagining became the dream, and the dream recurred
As the heat grew deeper and internal and in the darkest night
I glowed red unseen with the geothermal pressure that crushed me
Into fire deep beneath the earth. I awoke in those days
Unsteady, perplexed by my still-extant feet, legs, torso—that me.
I looked in the mirror. The days required shoveling snow, shopping
For food, listening to music. I was defiant. I began to imagine
The quartz, in all its permutations in dark and light, its molecular
Structure, and the feldspar, until by day I was talking to myself
Largely in chemical equations and by night, as I knew, the quartz
And feldspar began to conjoin in the extreme heat and my body
Burned down into the site of the thing to come. I waited.
It was time. I had had enough. Haven't you? Perhaps not.
That one night, lacking opioids, I took extra Remeron and Xanax
To stimulate unconsciousness and dreams, and there, finally,
The affirming volcanic fire: the change shook me as I convulsed,
Semi-conscious momentarily, knowing I was in bed but for the final
Time, not unwilling, though the body panicked, aware as bodies are
That it would die and death was its antithesis. Why do bodies
Resist? It was no longer my problem. Just there, perhaps a few
Hundred feet beneath Mount Saint Helens, just before I preserved
Being but lost self-awareness, the beauty of it: my own circular
Ruins. I had the mind of granite, which is no mind but the light
Implicit in the darkness, the volcanic furnace as the forge, enfolded
      wings.
Who is writing this? Some remnant trace, like a child who hides
      things.

RESIDUUM

§49. Absolute consciousness as the residuum
after the annihilation of the world—Edmund Husserl,
Ideas Pertaining to a Pure Phenomenology and to
a Phenomenological Philosophy, Volume One

And you wonder why "good-bye" is so difficult. . .This,
however you define "this," invariably is so much less—
you know. This is why we quarrel. Why I love you
and cannot prove it. Why a trip to Dylan Thomas'
boathouse in August might well be futile, or
the beginning. I find it comforting that a skylight
separates me now from the energy of the sun
and clouds fore-gathering in the air outside:
no question. The explosion has shown signs:
it will be monumental. And we won't, afterward,
care, although it will be sad, saying good-bye
to this little tragic messy corner of the universe,
with its sexual assaults and lilacs, its boys and girls
bleeding and the dogwoods in full bloom. But:
there we will be, finally, although not identifiable
to one another except by the markers we leave here,
outside the body, outside its consciousness. Here.

SIGHTINGS

I think Wallace Stevens believed he was right, for decades.
Then he began to believe something else—not lush
Or elaborate, no complacencies or artificers, but the
"Scrawny cry." The meager. The minor. The something
That was out there. It was all around him, each day,
Walking that twenty minutes back and forth
On his Hartford route. He noticed it in its bits,
The things no one particularly wanted. The things
No one particularly wanted took root in his mind
As an opposition, and sometimes he lamented,
In those last five years: "A fantastic effort has failed."
But more often he was curious. Sometimes learning late
That you are fundamentally wrong is a great gift. The scrawny
Things began to take root in his mind. He watched them move,
Late at night, with his secret Jameson's. They moved as they
Moved, not as he moved them, but they refused to give him up.
They were his. A couple of days before, he wrote them all down
In a poem of twelve lines. There was an edge he was about to cross.
Husserl might have objected at the phrasing "the end of the mind,"
But would have understood the concept. Was Stevens afraid?
I have seen the mortally ill in absolute terror of death, that turmoil.
I don't think Stevens was afraid at all. I think he was relieved.

THE INTERRUPTION

In the end, for that is how it seemed, she had almost consented. Do we all, in that last moment, accede with a will, even the violently taken? She did not know. Yet *altogether believing,* however incredulous, she oversaw the landscape as it presented itself, its simultaneous sunset and sunrise. How perfect. . .*But where are the trees?* And so she panicked and pulled back. *The trees had been mended, as an essential exercise/ In an inhuman meditation* would not be written for another 34 years, and even if it had been, would she have seen as mended something apparently entirely absent? How could she have been so wronged, how could each consciousness be so robbed of one thing, there at the end, that final consolation without which we do, yes, pull back, death is not for us, yet wrestling over the terrible realization that the dream had been real but so had its end, she heard the explosion of fireworks, the shouts and celebrations. The war had ended. And she had lived. And he had died. *Now there would be time for everything.* And she indeed would live long enough to know "The World as Meditation," to outlast it in her way by 36 more years. But she would never believe it. One fiction did not change the outcome of another, and neither fiction changed what was to come, what she could not leave behind, aside from her name, Katherine Anne Porter, and the foretellings of Faulkner, McCullers, O'Connor, and the trees that never returned.

CHANGES

I do not think that Edmund Husserl meant
In 1913 that consciousness would be eternal after
"the annihilation of the world." The residuum,
The one remaining "Real," never clearly attached
To the universe of birth and death, of its six
Chemical bases and its synaptic simulacrum. . .
But we don't know this, as we don't know
Why particles in nonbaryonic dark matter
Are "things" we can identify but not explain:
In a dying universe, however else the signs,
Consciousness, too, at the end, will die.
Are you frightened? Just as an intrusion
Into the void from an adjacent universe
Set ours in motion, you might imagine
We live a "version" of consciousness,
The greatest meta-story of them all:
While out there, among the stars we cannot
Detect without our own destruction, the other forms
Of being smear their being across their own creation,
Some knowing of themselves, some not,
And the latter not caring, as you should not care,
If you can, if you could follow Lucretius, if
You could, though love still heals, though love
Brings the well-fed to the table of the starving.

NEAR THE END

Because just there, when if there had been a high hill
You could have seen them, the midwestern troupe halted
For a declaration of beauty. None led nor followed, thus
No one was chosen to speak, and none did. They knew
By then to wait, to hear: it was enough that they had
Stopped, all that forward motion in what for most
Would be an unthinkably short time. *And what,* you
May ask indignantly in that twenty-first century way,
Is beauty, and why should it be the key, as opposed to measured,
Rational analysis? They were unimpressed. In the interim,
They knew what they had long discussed before,
That beauty disclosed itself only when it was ready,
That it was without paradigm, could not be theorized,
Occupied no category apart from what it upon revelation
Defined, did not without cause reveal itself. To those
Who might witness, it changed them, quieted—
Keats' urn, if you stop to consider it, invisible to us,
And that ode his only ode of its kind, "The Eve
Of Saint Agnes" by contrast an erotic poem—different,
Yes—but just then, there it was, across the sky like the last
Asteroid to hit the earth, extinction-level event—and—
Gone that fast. They turned back, then, to the car, for
Galveston, that thrilled, wounded city with its dreamland
Trash and its long, long view of the Gulf, the Gulf
Like a river with its source in northern Minnesota,
Running down past Iowa and so on and so on
To the Delta which existed only because it was home
To so many secrets of beauty, and then out into nowhere.

ACKNOWLEDGMENTS

Over the past 31 years, this work would not have been possible without the remarkable mothers of my six children—Nate, Georgia, Thomas, Hart, Peter, and Faye—and thus here I would like deeply to thank Lesley Wright, Laura Rigal, Rachel Sauter, Laura Crossett, and Elizabeth Wisnosky.

I also wish to thank the publications in which some of these poems previously appeared: *Now,* Saint Julian Press; the *Atlantic;* the *New Republic;* the *Southern Review;* the *Threepenny Review; Occident; Prairie Schooner;* the *Christian Science Monitor;* and *The Uncommon Touch: Fiction and Poetry from the Stanford Writing Workshop,* ed. John L'Heureux (Stanford, CA: Stanford Alumni Association, 1989).

Ron Starbuck, the publisher and CEO of Saint Julian Press, Houston, has been an exceptionally patient and able editor and friend throughout this process. My debt to him remains profound.

ABOUT THE AUTHOR

Thomas Simmons taught for 24 years in the Department of English at the University of Iowa; in the spring of 2016 he started something new and has been writing ever since. Before that, he was an assistant and associate professor in the Program in Writing and Humanistic Studies at the Massachusetts Institute of Technology; before that, he was a doctoral student in English at the University of California, Berkeley, a Wallace Stegner Fellow in Creative Writing at Stanford, and a Stanford University undergraduate. His seven previous books, one of which (*The Unseen Shore: Memories of a Christian Science Childhood*, Beacon Press, 1991) caused some offense in Boston, may be viewed at amazon.com site listed below. He lives in Grinnell, Iowa.

Visit his Amazon author page at: *amazon.com/author/Thomas Simmons.*

TYPEFACE: Perpetua Titling MT

The half title and title pages are set in the typeface Perpetua Titling MT for the book's title. Perpetua is a serif typeface designed by English sculptor and stonemason Eric Gill for the British Monotype Corporation at around 1925, when Gill's reputation as a leading artist-craftsman was high.

TYPEFACE: GARAMOND – Garamond

The poems in this book are set in the typeface Garamond, named for the sixteenth-century Parisian engraver Claude Garamont. The font was originally designed in 1530 by printer Robert Estienne.